To the Person Who Tends My Body

poems by

Michael Meyerhofer

Finishing Line Press
Georgetown, Kentucky

To the Person Who Tends My Body

Publisher: Leah Huete de Maines
Editor: Christen Kincaid
Cover Art: Ugur Tandogan via Pexels
Author Photo: James Mostek
Cover Design: Elizabeth Maines McCleavy

Order online: www.finishinglinepress.com
also available on amazon.com

Author inquiries and mail orders:
Finishing Line Press
PO Box 1626
Georgetown, Kentucky 40324
USA

Table of Contents

I lie awake; I have become
like a bird alone on a roof.
—Psalm 102:7

URBAN LEGEND

My father sat me down to tell me
not about the secret powers of women
nor my mother's failing kidneys

but a story he'd just heard: a boy my age
vacationing with family in Mexico,
a boy who saw his kid-sister abducted

and gave chase through a throng
of brown bodies. How the parents,
when they noticed the absence,

sought the help of border guards
with eagles on their sleeves—
strong, faceless men who knew

it was already too late. An hour later,
the kids turned up with their guts
scooped out, replaced with narcotics

the cartel tried to smuggle across
a border bristling with rifles and flags.
In real life, I didn't have a sister

and we never vacationed anywhere
that took more than an hour to reach.
Still, I worried myself sick

imagining pills, powder, plants,
that tug-o-war on my insides,
wondered whether those bags of sin

lied flat like deflated balloons
or bulged like the moony breasts
of women I saw in magazines,

women with eyes like damp gravestones
who leaned on men with muscles
that spoke their own language.

FOR AHMAUD ARBERY, AN UNARMED BLACK JOGGER KILLED FOR ALLEGEDLY LOOKING IN THE WINDOW OF A HOUSE UNDER CONSTRUCTION

I was twenty-two, white, in love
that day I wasn't shot for trespassing.

It happened nearly two decades ago.
We started out in the backseat

of her parents' oxblood Subaru,
heading back from the country club

with bellies full of prime rib
and vegetables I could not name.

Then her father touched the brake,
pointed to a mansion being built

beyond a phalanx of dogwoods,
timbers stacked like wine-washed

bones on a generous plot of Iowa soil.
The crews had already gone home,

just some golden tape left behind.
So we pulled over, got out, explored—

her father darkly pinstriped, her mother
sporting a heavy rosary of pearls.

Before long, neighbors spotted us
and waved, smiling from their hoses.

Unfazed, my girlfriend and I
slipped away and touched primally

in what might have been a stranger's
future bedroom, its walls unmade.

After a great while, we reunited
beside half a staircase. Her parents

forgave our absence with a shrug
and the suggestion of frozen yogurt.

On the way back, I could smell her
on my fingers, which made her blush.

Meanwhile, her parents shared
daydreams of their own mansion

with taller floors and windows,
thicker drapes to block the sunset.

WATCHING LIONS SPARE A TURTLE ON THE SAME DAY
THAT DEREK CHAUVIN WAS FOUND GUILTY OF MURDER

My friend sends me the video:
lions kneeling at a watering hole,

chins speckled in blood,
just trying to rinse it all down

beneath a sun that whitens
anything it can't burn.

Then this turtle paddles up
and starts licking their beards,

their jaws, like it can't stop
tasting another's hunger.

For a moment, tongues wrestle.
Then, somehow, it happens:

the terrapin swims clear,
lions exit on claws like triggers,

and it costs us nothing to forget
what graffities the dry grass—

the zebra with its torn flanks,
the sentence of bleached bones.

FOR MY BROTHER

I.

Again I return to that leaning barn of whitewash
and wind-warped rafters, weathervane that never spun,

rim-rust that rejected our free-throws and hovered,
a ratty halo, over the tenuous forts of February—

so much repacked snowmelt shadowed by that
squatters' shack where they fought over how long

our mother would outlast a rural doc's diagnosis.
When in my seventh year they came with stretchers

and sirens, we waited in the truck. You distracted me
with the atlas from the glove box, how finely it unfolded

like all the tomorrows I sensed were not to come.
But it's the barn I remember, whistling like a cavity

at the end of our drive. And most of all, that you
heard it, too. That you heard it, but did not flinch.

II.

Ragweed that grew around silos, dead snakes
between turnip rows, the gnats who rose in waves

from the knife-edge of sun and field: all these
went before us. So, too, she who clipped coupons

and made us wear our stocking caps no matter
how it mussed our hair. Brother, I lied when I said

I didn't notice the baby's fist of your lymph nodes,
over-swell of white blood cells roused to fight

what isn't there. This is the only way I know
to repay you: to hide my dumb lies, and this poem,

and these pagan tears, until the last barn owl
shrivels to dust and it no longer matters to do so.

SCAVENGERS

I want to write a poem that ends
with rain but I know better
and besides, I've done that already.
So I'll just tell you of the house
my father tore down, how he broke
through plaster and floorboards,
hauling out tarnished copper
to sell for my mother's insulin
and the diapers my spine required.

How one day he brought me along
to ferry buckets and a thermos
he ordered me not to taste.
Other men had already taken
their turns with hammers and saws
and the house looked
like it came from a war movie,
scattered with nails and gaps
leading all the way to the basement.

How seeing it made me think
not of endless hospital visits
or bodies left open
on the television screen,
but jars of playground crickets
with a punctured lid, like
we were helping the house breathe.
Long boards bridging end to end,
nothing left to hold onto.

Be careful, my father said,
in a voice that spoke of thirst.
And I did, inching along
until he caught me by the belt
and hauled me the rest of the way.
I was afraid, I looked down,
but I made it anyway. I thought
this would make me brave.
But I was only following orders.

A BELATED APOLOGY TO A TRANSGENDER COLLEAGUE

I still regret the time I high-fived a guy
who was halfway through
physically becoming a woman
and even said something terribly
heteromasculine like *Right on, dude!*
in answer to her praise
of a book we both loved. I meant it
to sound friendly and supportive,
so secure in my Midwestern liberality
that I almost missed the hesitation
in her eyes before she returned
the gesture—our bare palms
touching like shadows, the digits mirrored—
not to mention the scowls
of other colleagues at the table.
Then, a month later, attending a gala
alongside her and her wife, I walked up
and said, *Hello, ladies,*
thinking that would absolve me,
though even in my ears the words
sounded off kilter, due not
to insincerity but nerves, my own inability
to stand anyone thinking badly of me.
True, this isn't about my own
rotten childhood, but I seem
unable to speak as anybody but myself.
There's one other moment I return to:
walking by her office a few days
after my latest verbal idiocy
to ask how she'd been. She mentioned
a forthcoming operation, a little
catch in her voice, and in my haste
to commiserate, I said, *Oh, I have one of those
coming up, too,* merely referring
to a bit of dental work,
though her eyes widened
a split second before she said,
Well, man, good luck, and meant it.

MY MOTHER'S AUTOPSY

A man with a Scottish accent
calls to say he's found
a blank verse sonnet in her rib cage,
folded up like a love letter.
But I can hardly express
my disbelief before he moves on
to the haiku on the underside
of her eyelids, the pantoum
bracketed in vertebrae,
a rather bawdy limerick buried
in the saccharine junkyard
of her kidneys. *I didn't know*,
I say, as he lauds the ode
wreathing her navel, the erasure
where her thighs meet. He lowers
his voice, says he knows
we've asked to get her back
in ash-form, offers to read some
before feeding the rest to fire.
But this is where it ends,
thanks to the alarm clock
spurring me down the freeway
with the sun in my eyes.
So many exits before the real one.
Still, I can feel her beside me,
saying nothing, except to apologize
every time a bump causes
her arm to brush against mine.

THE GENDER REVOLUTION, TELEVISED

Hard to believe, but there they were
on the ultrasounds—bowties, bowties everywhere,
shoelace knots beneath fetal chins.
The CDC swept in, all urgent and scowly
behind their respirators. In some cases,
expectant mothers confessed to cigarettes
and half-glasses of merlot when
nobody was looking. Others blamed
excessive yoga or that latest fad
in supplements (organic, expensive, hard
to pronounce). Still others tried to look
on the bright side, joking that now,
they'd have to pick up a baseball glove
on their way home. But upon closer inspection,
sonograms revealed just as many clefts
as peninsulas. And before long, websites
sprang up disparaging everything
from nuclear power plants to a recent box
office flop on the military exploits of James Gray
(born Hannah Snell, Worchester, England, 1723).
Still, their hearts beat like tiny, dapper
whales adrift in amniotic ether. Months passed.
Presidents and prime ministers made speeches
calling for restraint and goodwill.
Churches, temples, mosques all blazed
with candles. But labors passed
without major incident. Once the nurses
hosed them off—those squalling enigmas,
those downsized Chippendales—the ties
came off with just a tug. Newborns
hardly noticed. Meanwhile, thousands
ended up in laboratories where microscopes
revealed nothing but crisscrossing lines
of silk. Others got thrown in the trash or burned
by frightened, backyard vigilantes.
But that left millions for the baby books,
glued down like charcoal butterflies—
proof that for one whole year, it happened.
Then teeth, then grades.
Pages that never seemed to lie flat,
no matter how hard we pressed.

WHAT MY GRANDMOTHER TAUGHT ME

If you have animals, feed them
all your table scraps—wheat-crusts
soaked in grease and gravy,
crumpled rags of chicken-skin,
that dark knot of bone
in every pork-steak. There's no
such thing as cannibalism, just life
circling back around. Pray often.
Expect no reply. Start each morning
with coffee so strong, only vinegar
can thin the inevitable stain.
Keep a diary. Sweep daily
and you'll never need to vacuum.
Alcoholics are like stray cats
that cannot be rid of fleas.
If you choose to be a gardener
and people want to shake your hand,
they should expect to get dirty.
Learn the names of flowers,
how to separate cherry blossoms
from honeysuckle even
in the heady tang of manuring.
When you open canned vegetables,
that hiss of air means nothing
soured while you were away.
Mind your cellar. Rain is not a bath.
Iron rusts. Wood lasts longer
than plastic. Drink tea only
when you can't sleep. Render fat
to make your own suet cakes
to keep songbirds in the boughs.
That way, the sky won't forget you.
The best dryer is a clothesline,
but always check the folds
for sleeping butterflies. It matters
not at all where each pan goes,
just that they be returned
where they can be found later.
Funerals aren't the place to grieve.
If ice hides the highway while
you're tending an infant, a diaper

can be fashioned out of rags
and an old bread-bag but remember
to rinse away the crumbs. In time,
everything hardens into glass.
It doesn't matter what you write,
just that you wrote something
and signed it. Be ready
to readjust the antenna. Mourn
even the best trade because it means
something was given up. Wars
aren't the only events
that leave you feeling like
an unmade bed. Soup should
simmer until carrots and onions
and bone-broth hang like dewdrops
from the ceiling. If your crackers
go stale, you can crisp them
in the oven. Remember me
if it's not too much of a hassle.

DEAR DAUGHTER

I know you don't exist
but say we were halfway back
from seeing a friend
in a bullet-smooth casket
and you asked what to expect
if there really is no God,
no passing like water
mouth to mouth,
and I told you in the car
between one tree-named sign
and the next the worst
case scenario: when we die,
we pass into nothingness,
that same shapeless garden
from whence you came,
like the darkness in a vase
we filled with milk and light.
Or, put another way,
I'm not afraid of being eaten
by whatever gave us you.

SECOND GRADE

One late afternoon, riding the bus,
I turned and saw a boy about my age

lying in a driveway, not moving,
likely just pretending though I feared

he was hurt and had no idea how
to call for help. Days passed

without mention of a dead boy
so eventually I forgave my silence,

that lump like an acorn already
stretching my heart in two.

But I still remember him lying there,
arms splayed like cast-off sticks,

chin frightfully angled, no mother
scowling from a foreign porch.

Maybe now, he's holding a bottle
in a baby's mouth, threading a bullet

through the snowy hide of a deer.
Maybe we've passed each other

and didn't know it. Maybe it's you.
And mine is the face that blurred by

just as you looked up and waved,
too late, and ran back inside.

GO BIG OR GO HOME

Here come the ones who chose
the second option, advancing

across the sad freeways of America
on their way to not a damn

thing worth carving in stone. Still,
see how they white-knuckle

the steering wheel, the cracked grill
burping through rush-hour traffic

and a slow-tumbling sun
that reddens the windshield

as though pelting it with tomatoes.
They know that tomorrow, too,

they will eat from a microwave.
That life is mostly for pushing

numbers from column to column
so the electricity stays on

and all your children can flee,
and pets who are even more helpless

and closer to death will stay
grateful for the cans

you open with fingers that must
seem to them like magic.

COMMERCIAL BREAK

When the TV detective says how bad it is
for a guy to reach middle age without
having a family, I realize he's talking to me,

pausing halfway through his investigation
into a cultish double-murder to present
his tough but fair critique of all

the relationships I've failed to buttress
like a fortress during the Crusades.
True, we don't even know each other,

and the irony is that said detective is busy
taking a shotgun to his own marriage
just as so many of my old friends

seem to be doing these days,
if late night texts are any indication.
Still, I'm not sure I was right to trade

unconditional love for steaks and cat litter,
which are the two things I just bought
at midnight from the corner store

because I felt like it, and also
if you really want to know, because
of the silence between rooms—

which is not like the silence before
catapults or a gunshot, or even
the silence before the birth-scream:

all that muck and nudity, nurses
rushing in with towels, loved ones
crowding in beside people

you don't much care for and normally
wouldn't address, let alone embrace
save on these special occasions.

STATE OF THE UNION

All the news is talking
about the lack of surgical masks
and ice cream trucks for the dead,
how many grandfathers
need help to breathe,
but today, I can't seem to stop
wondering how oranges smell
when they're burning.
For that, too, is something
I've never known, having missed
my one chance to walk
a few blocks to a supermarket
that caught fire years ago,
the hoses too late, asparagus
like kindling, cans of pasta sauce
popping like firecrackers
they say, though men will say
anything to make up
for what they can't buy or steal:
wine bottles boiled dry,
rotisserie chickens charred
down to the size of a child's fist,
a forest of Bible-ply burnt
before it can even assist
those places we keep hidden,
and everywhere, puddles
of plastic flowing mercurially
between shelves that topple
whether you're looking or not.
But had I risen at the first sound,
the first engine's wail
lancing through my hangover,
I, too, might have stood so close
that every apolitical shift
in the night breeze taught me
something new about dairy aisles,
snap peas heat-forged
into arrowheads, and oranges:
what sweet mist they offer,
wept from the inside out.

IF COUCHES HAD SPHINCTERS

That means, like us, they are born
with mouths that need feeding.

It doesn't matter that we can't see them.
How often have we pulled open

their guts to find the remote control
they mistook for mother's milk?

Sweet Christ, how they suffer:
all those shocks of spilled coffee,

chip crumbs like shards of glass,
toothy bouquets of house keys.

For us, they wreck their spines.
They sit naked in the dark, waiting.

And still we leave them on street corners
amidst all that dust and rain

without so much as an apology,
never mind how we'll feel later

as we sweep up the mess they used
every inch of their bodies to hide.

THE SHAPESHIFTER IN THERAPY FOR SURVIVOR'S GUILT

First time I saw her, she was crying in a pharmacy.
I transformed into a puppy and licked her ankles.

She kicked me, pointed out the absence of consent
and threatened to call the cops. True, she had a point,

but later when I became a scattering of rose petals
across her windshield, I thought I saw her smile

before she turned the wipers on. It was tough
spelling out my apology in the clouds—I'd never

stretched myself that far—but I meant it.
That Friday, I let her ride me through the park,

then became a butterfly and kissed her forehead.
She texted later, said she was lonely but didn't

want to rush things so I became the rain
and pattered off the eaves until she fell asleep.

Soon, she started to have fun with it: *Show me
a baby goat, a pterodactyl, a giraffe with flippers.*

She even made videos for her family—her
playing badminton with Virginia Woolf,

cooking a grilled cheese with Abraham Lincoln.
I started to wonder why she never asked to see

my true self. Sometimes, lying next to her,
I'd change back and wait for her to wake up

and run away, screaming. Every time
she stirred, though, I'd become a quilt

that smelled like her favorite perfume.
But it turns out she liked me best as water.

Days she didn't want to talk, I'd just
fill the bathtub and let her soak in me,

flowing over her scars like I was
pouring down the rungs of a ladder.

EPILOGUE OF THE CHOSEN ONE

One day, you're trying to kill a shapeshifter
with a spork or dangling from a chopper
that's spiraling into a live volcano.
The next, you're fiddling with the guts
of a station wagon or asking drunk teenagers
to upgrade their Super Slammy Meal.
You try to keep that edge by tiring yourself out
with pushups then assembling handguns
blindfolded. But you can't
outrun the truth as easily as you did
that squad of transdimensional cyborgs:
the world doesn't need you anymore.
The last hellmouth sealed, the mothership
tricked into a blackhole, burgeoning
artificial intelligence persuaded to choose
cupcakes over nuclear warheads.
Still, you're trying your best
to fix your tie in this gas station mirror,
wondering why no one responds
to your dating profile. Maybe in time
the president will call to say thanks
but right now, you're late for the funeral,
the grand opening, the last meeting
before a new sales quarter. And just like that
you spot her in the parking lot:
that mysterious brunette who wants
absolutely nothing to do with you.
Only she's lost her keys,
and in less time than it took you
to escape Purgatory, she wants to know
how you learned to hotwire cars.
She sidles closer. You smell flowers.
Her eyes gleam like shell casings.
But you walk away, unsure where to start.

SILVER-BACKED CHEVROTAIN, WITH FANGS AND HOOVES, PHOTOGRAPHED IN WILD FOR FIRST TIME —NPR Headline, Nov. 11, 2019

Schoolkids all over the country
keep pace with TV cameras

by practicing a new word—*impeach*—
even as a dozen time zones

from the leaning pillars of democracy,
unseen for decades, a silver-

splashed deer with fangs
tiptoes out of the undergrowth

and presses his nose to the lens,
two unlit moons kissing

in the wild gaps between rivers.
Why should these days matter?

Bones are just the bones
of whatever else came before:

a quickening of dust into rock,
into fire, into blood, then

a softening of God into rain.
See how each drop opens

like luggage, how a heart can only
be a heart if it dies screaming?

Meanwhile, the chevrotain
moves about on hooves

so thin, the mind recalls
the ankles of a ballet dancer,

the stick-limbs of a cave painting.
Even those fangs, used

to fight over mates, only led
to a thickening of muscles

around the throat. We repeat
what we know. Each generation

an untamed refrain you need
not sing, unless you want to.

RETURNING THE FAVOR

As the story goes, my grandmother
found me face-down, blue-lipped,

about the size of a leaky football,
the long drive to the hospital still dark

and thick with ice, so she cleared
my airways and sat with me

until dawn crisped the snowy oaks,
checking my throat as one might

an overwrought toaster. Strange
that I hadn't heard this before,

never amongst all those tales
of surgeries and deadweight casts,

like she'd decided to save this one
for my last visit home when

she recounts it twice, perfectly,
each unchanged detail like an oath

I feel I am supposed to memorize.
At first, I think it's so I'll know

how much she cares, picture her
serene as a Catholic saint,

her whole skull aglow. But then,
when I find myself pacing outside

her bedroom door, leaning in,
listening hour upon glacial hour

to her wavering rasp, I realize
she meant how awful it is to love,

and of course, what it means
that we go on loving anyway.

THE PROTESTS OF THE UNWASHED MASSES

Not once have I witnessed it:
the calculation that must proceed
every rotten cabbage,
every egg launched like Greek fire
at some dumb passing noble
pilloried for his misdeeds.
But I like to imagine the mob
gathering reasonably that morning
at their separate tables, so many
fruits of the garden laid out
in that first slant of light,
their stomachs still rumbling
from an inadequate breakfast.
Perhaps they called in
the children to help them decide
which radish was too far gone,
which turnip would be better thrown
than mashed into a bitter stew.
Later, there will be shouting,
lips glistening with spittle.
But for now, they turn each apple
in their hands, like a judge.
Which one looks sick?
Which one can still be saved?

AFTER HEARING A CONGRESSMAN BLAME BIRTH DEFECTS ON UNHEALTHY LIVING

To be fair, I partied a lot as a zygote,
shotgunning so many beers it's no wonder
my spine wouldn't straighten. Later,
as a blastocyst, I got blasted on tequila
until half my right ear dissolved
in a fog of lousy decisions.
As an embryo, thick-headed
despite being gelatinous, I transformed
my amniotic sac into a dance club
and inhaled enough cocaine for two
decades of spasms to pass through
my innards like electroshocks.
But that's nothing compared
to the fetus stage, where believe it
or not, I stood on my head for months
and spent all day listening to the drumbeats
of a woman whose name I did not know.
By then, I'd gotten hooked
on meditation and an all-liquid diet
but you can only hum for so long
before you wear a hole in your throat
like the one my doctors had to stitch up,
along with the feet I broke
body-surfing toward the light.

TEXT MESSAGE BETWEEN WILDFIRES

I wanted to tell you about the clouds,
how they moved like sign language

over the freeway this afternoon,
momentarily shading great swaths

of knuckle-to-knuckle traffic from
a sun already bruised by carelessness,

hinting at some other world
woven into ours the way physicists

say there are dozens more dimensions
upholding the bones of our reality.

Only autocorrect changed it to cows,
and so for the rest of the day

as I worried between errands,
I imagined mottled herds floating by,

flipping their county-sized tails,
their throats ringing like church bells.

VIRTUE SIGNALING

While millions of us are watching
two old white men yell at each other
in a country where the dead fill enough
coffins to crowd sixty football fields,
an article appears in my newsfeed
describing how a teenage girl
got her nose and lips cut off
some twelve centuries ago. I imagine
the world was different back when
she was walking and not lying
in the stuffy British earth, her skull
packed in soil like a teacup. They say
it could have been punishment
for adultery, that she was buried
outside the cemetery—a final insult—
a while after they opened her
face like a birthday card envelope.
No mention if she ever missed
the smell of burnt bread and candles
shaped from tallow, how she felt
afterwards navigating a maze
of untrampled wildflowers,
one stem tucked behind her ear.

TO THE PERSON WHO TENDS MY BODY

Probably you'll never know
that I wrote this especially for you.
First, I'm sorry—shouldn't
we always say that
when we can't undress ourselves?
I won't be offended if you flinch
at my cockeyed toes
and missing ear, a pantheon
of scars I can't explain. Strange
to be there with you
and also, to not be there. Still,
thank you for your service
though I bet it strains you
even later, driving to the coast
where the sun twists itself
into a burning lollipop.
I hope your salary is adequate,
that someone makes you feel
like a helium balloon
rising out an open window.
Don't feel bad if you miss a button.
Thank you for your hands,
how they did what I could not.

ACKNOWLEDGMENTS

2River View—"Second Grade"

American Journal of Poetry—"The Protests of the Unwashed Masses"

Atlanta Review—"The Shapeshifter in Therapy for Survivor's Guilt"

Asimov's Science Fiction Magazine—"Epilogue of the Chosen One"

Comstock Review—"Virtue Signaling"

Crab Orchard Review—"Urban Legend"

FRiGG—"Scavengers" and "If Couches Had Sphincters"

Hayden's Ferry Review—"The Gender Revolution, Televised"

Hobart—"Go Big or Go Home"

MAYDAY—"State of the Union"

Mid-American Review—"Text Message Between Wildfires"

Missouri Review—"Dear Daughter"

National Poetry Review—"A Belated Apology to a Transgender Colleague" and "To the Person Who Tends My Body"

Natural Bridge—"Commercial Break"

Rattle—"For Ahmaud Arbery, an Unarmed Black Jogger Killed for Allegedly Looking in the Window of a House Under Construction," "Silver-Backed Chevrotain, With Fangs And Hooves, Photographed In Wild For First Time," and "Watching Lions Spare a Turtle on the Same Day that Derek Chauvin was Found Guilty of Murder"

River Styx—"My Mother's Autopsy"

South Dakota Review—"After Hearing a Congressman Blame Birth Defects on Unhealthy Living"

Southern Review—"What My Grandmother Taught Me"

Tupelo Quarterly—"For My Brother"

"A Belated Apology to a Transgender Colleague" also appeared on *Verse Daily*.

"For Ahmaud Arbery, an Unarmed Black Jogger Killed for Allegedly Looking in the Window of a House Under Construction," "Urban Legend," "A Belated Apology to a Transgender Colleague," "My Mother's Autopsy," "State of the Union," and "If Couches Had Sphincters" also appeared in *Aeolian Harp Anthology* Vol. 7.

Michael Meyerhofer is the author of five books and six chapbooks of poetry, along with two fantasy trilogies. He has received the James Wright Poetry Award, the Liam Rector First Book Award, the Brick Road Poetry Book Prize, the Laureate Prize for Poetry, and other honors. He also serves as the Poetry Editor of *Atticus Review*. His work has appeared in an eclectic list of journals including *The Sun, Fantasy and Science Fiction Magazine, Southern Review, Rattle, Asimov's Science Fiction Magazine, Ninth Letter,* and others. For more information and an embarrassing childhood photo, visit troublewithhammers.com.